Your Story Starts Here.
Title:

____

____

By:____________________________________

Made in the USA
Middletown, DE
12 December 2023

45534350R00126